THE PENGUIN CLASSICS

EDITED BY E. V. RIEU

L 76

Property of
Charles A. Owen Jr.
Medieval Studies Library

TWO SATYR PLAYS

Euripides' *Cyclops*

AND

Sophocles' *Ichneutai*

TRANSLATED
WITH AN INTRODUCTION BY
Roger Lancelyn Green

PENGUIN BOOKS

Penguin Books Ltd, Harmondsworth, Middlesex
U.S.A.: Penguin Books Inc., 3300 Clipper Mill Road, Baltimore 11, Md
AUSTRALIA: Penguin Books Pty Ltd, 762 Whitehorse Road,
Mitcham, Victoria

—

First published 1957

Copyright © Roger Lancelyn Green, 1957

*The terms for the performance of these plays may be
obtained from the League of Dramatists, 84 Drayton
Gardens, London, SW 10, to whom all applications for
permission should be made*

Made and printed in Great Britain
by William Clowes and Sons, Limited
London and Beccles

TO
*Daphne and Robert
Levens*

CONTENTS

INTRODUCTION

In all the rich and varied legacy of ancient Greek literature, there is perhaps no item that has come down to us more curious than the Satyr Play. Its beginnings are those of Drama itself, and it may have existed before Tragedy was invented.

The earliest elements of drama are thought to have sprung from the fertility dance on the threshing-floor when the harvest was ended and the cycle of life about to be renewed. It was a serious occasion, vital to the life of the little community, sacrificial and reverential, but also physical and illustrative of the natural primitive instincts towards the new generation of corn, of cattle, and of man.

These rites, growing out of the magic ritual of a semi-civilized village society, began with the dance and the invocation or charm; they celebrated and illustrated the desire and the pursuit of fecundity – simply, often crudely, but in a spirit of reverence.

This developed into, or was accompanied by, an obscure production called a 'Dithyramb', of which no early example has survived. It seems to have been a choric song, accompanied by some ritual movement in the form of a dance.

What relation this bore to the Athenian drama, and how Tragedy grew out of it, or out of the Dithyramb alone, is one of the problems which scholars are still discussing. The steps are obscure, only the result is certain. We do not even know whether Demeter, the corn-goddess, was ever concerned with either, and if so, how Dionysus came to take her place.

He was a late-comer to Olympus, and probably of Asiatic origin. The myths made him the son of Zeus by Semele, princess of Thebes in Boeotia, north-west of Athens; but her father, Cadmus, was a Phoenician prince from Asia Minor. Dionysus, or Bacchus, brought the gift of the vine to mankind, taught them to make wine – and inevitably, to get drunk. The Bacchic ecstasy was produced by this wonderful gift of Dionysus, and his followers were naturally much addicted to it. They were the wild women, Maenads or Bacchants, probably a relic of the orgiastic rites of the Asiatic priestesses of the cult – and the Satyrs.

9

These strange creatures seem to have been more Greek than oriental. They are mentioned by the early mythographer Hesiod as the brothers of the Nymphs, and are described by him as 'idle and worthless'; probably they began as minor nature-deities. Silenus himself started out as a water-spirit in Asia Minor; at first he was the maker of springs and fountains, later his special duty was to see that the vines were well-watered, and he very soon took to drink, and replaced the contents of his water-skin with wine. He was already an attendant of Dionysus, and when the Satyrs also joined his following, Silenus was recognized as their father. His own ancestry was obscure, though later writers try to associate him with Pan.

But the Satyrs and Silenus were never goat-legged. They had bristly hair, broad noses, pointed ears, even tails – but that was all. They are primitive and semi-wild, the natural as opposed to the civilized man. Their characteristics are the curiosity of the unsophisticated savage, and his acquisitiveness, together with the undisciplined lusts of those not subject to ages of refinement and cultured repression. In a lost play by Aeschylus of which a few fragments remain, it appears that the Satyrs attempt to kiss the flames of the first fire which Prometheus kindles on earth after he has stolen the divine spark from Olympus. When wine is to be had, they drink to excess; in danger they are flagrant cowards; they will steal, and lie, and boast quite innocently, and are, in fact, completely amoral.

Though the dance and song on the threshing-floor may at first have been in honour of Demeter, the Dithyramb seems always to have celebrated Dionysus, and Dionysus continued to be the patron of the Drama; the earliest plays were concerned with some incident in the legend of Dionysus himself, and his wanderings over the earth in company with the Satyrs and the Maenads.

It is not known exactly when and how Tragedy became separated from this original dramatic tradition, but it certainly did so, and grew speedily into the art-form which gave us the dramas of Aeschylus, Sophocles, and Euripides, the best of whose tragedies have scarcely been surpassed by any later dramatist.

But Tragedy, though it grew away from the original Satyric Drama, did not supplant it. In the Dionysia, the great dramatic festival at Athens, a Satyr play was performed after every three tragedies. It was sometimes, when the three tragedies formed a trilogy, even connected with them in subject or in characters.

Thus we have the unique example of a primitive drama continuing to exist side by side with the highest literary achievement; of the greatest dramatists writing what are almost folk-plays as well as their great tragedies; our two surviving examples were first performed at much the same date as Sophocles' *Antigone* (440 B.C.). It is almost as if Shakespeare had written a *Punch and Judy* show to be presented as an after-piece to *Romeo and Juliet*. But the example is not quite accurate, for the Satyr play continued to have some religious significance, though it is not certain how much. The nearest approach in our dramatic tradition is to be found in the medieval Miracle Plays: the shrewish humours of Noah's wife; the comic element of the thieving shepherd who afterwards kneels with all reverence in the stable at Bethlehem; or in the burlesque devil complete with horns and tail.

By the time of Sophocles and Euripides the most obvious function of the Satyr play was to supply a release from the tragic tension of the preceding plays, and in time the Satyr play might even be replaced by what we might call a romantic play such as *Alcestis* or *Helena*.

But the general relationship between the two kinds of drama remained very little altered, and the Satyr play never came to be grouped or associated with Comedy proper; either with the burlesque and slapstick variety raised to such a high level of literary and dramatic excellence by Aristophanes, or the comedy more in the modern sense which evolved out of this, when political satire was banned and a few ideas from the more romantic types of tragedy were added to the remains by Menander. (It should be stressed that there is no relation of any kind between the words 'satyr' and 'satire'.)

In style and theme the Satyr play never deviated very far from Tragedy, even if its spirit and much of its content might strike us now as more nearly allied to comedy, burlesque, or even farce.

The tragic diction, for example, was still used to some extent, Silenus and the Satyrs alone departing from it at all markedly; and they were the only characters in this type of play whose behaviour could be described as farcical. Thus Odysseus in *The Cyclops* retains most of his heroic character, and though Polyphemus is far from being the dreadful ogre of Homer's epic, he cannot quite be described as a figure of fun: they are, in fact, reduced from epic to fairy-tale stature – the Crafty Prince and the Thick-witted Giant.

Silenus and the Satyrs, however, exhibit all the characteristics of burlesque or farcical figures as we would understand the term; and their determination to be on the winning side and to profess their exaggerated allegiance to the person in power sets them well in the comic tradition. Though there is a big gap in the family tree, we cannot help feeling that in some way Silenus is the ancestor of Thraso and Bobadil, of Parolles and Joxer Daly.

And in what remains to us of the *Ichneutai* (the 'Searchers' or 'Trackers') of Sophocles, the only other example of a Satyr play we possess except for fragments of a few lines, the same characteristics are evident. Silenus is presented as Euripides presents him: a grasping, cowardly braggart, ready to betray either side, and yet a likeable rogue rather than a villain: 'a good sort, but a bad lot', as Andrew Lang said of Mary Stuart. Both Euripides and Sophocles make this quite clear: a Satyr is not an ordinary human being, and allowances must be made; for, after all, he is merely being himself.

Kyllene the nymph is a figure of almost full tragic dignity; she has more of it, indeed, than Odysseus; if he is the 'Wily Lad' of fairy-tale, she is very much the Princess; she lifts the whole play near to the 'pro-satyric' drama, such as *Alcestis*, which sometimes took the place of the Satyr play. Apollo, on the other hand, though his language is mainly in the diction of Tragedy, seems to lack dignity (perhaps on account of the triviality of so much that he says) just as Polyphemus fails to produce any sense of fear or horror. No great licence is required to present the angry and affronted god as petulant and a trifle spoilt, or the Cyclops as the traditionally stupid giant of most folk-tales.

In my version of the two plays I have stressed the burlesque element rather more, perhaps, than my texts strictly allow. By doing so I have striven to present the effect of the Satyr play: the light-hearted easing of tension after the Tragedies, and the naturalness, almost the earthiness, of a holiday in the Arcadian world of the Satyrs. Of all things a Satyr play should seem neither dull nor pedantic; the language should be simple, and at times at least as colloquial as a Gilbertian lyric.

This is certainly true if the Satyr plays are to be acted. Shelley's classic version of *The Cyclops* seems quite unsuitable for presentation, and Sir John Sheppard gave point to this fact when he made his acting version of the play in 1923 a mere adaptation in very racy English.

I have tried to strike a happy medium between the two methods. I have treated *The Cyclops* less reverently than did Shelley, whose blank verse is fairly literal, though his choruses are rather freely rendered. But mine, though free, is still a translation rather than an adaptation; it is a version 'of' and not 'after' Euripides: accurate even if not literal.

The Searching Satyrs presents a different problem. The papyrus which represents the only text was dug up in Egypt early this century and published for the first time in 1912. It suffers from a number of small gaps in the text, and one large one; in most cases it is easy to see how many lines are missing, and sometimes even to gather clues from odd words remaining as to what is lost. Two plays by Menander, recovered in much the same condition, have been superbly translated by Professor Gilbert Murray, who in doing so restored or filled in the gaps in his originals so as to present complete plays for the English reader. I have tried to do the same service to the remains of the Sophocles play, since gaps in dialogue and plot detract from most people's enjoyment – and would prevent the play from appearing on the stage. Following Professor Murray's august example, I have also refrained from dotting my version with square brackets and notes to indicate where I have supplied half-a-dozen lines, or where a half-line is indecipherable in the papyrus. I have, however, stated in the notes (otherwise of mythological and geographical allusions), printed at the end of the play, where the one big gap occurs which I have had the temerity to reconstruct entirely. Readers may like to guess where in the play this is before turning up the note; those anxious to probe deeper will find the Greek text, with an excellent prose version by Professor Denys Page, in the volume of the Loeb Classical Library called *Greek Literary Papyri*. Greekless readers anxious to pursue the fascinating pastime of comparing versions will find the only prose translation of *The Cyclops* in one of the Euripides volumes in the old Bohn Library, now very hard to find; but they have their choice of verse interpretations by Shelley, A. S. Way, and J. T. Sheppard.

But in translating both these plays and in completing the second, my main object has been to communicate my own delight in this strange and neglected art form, the Satyr Play. Our two surviving examples are far too little known, and we have been given small opportunity of appreciating them. *The Cyclops* has several amateur performances to its credit – in Greek, or in Sir John Sheppard's paraphrase – but *The Searching Satyrs* has still to stage its first revival for over two thousand years.

May, 1957   R. L. G.

THE CYCLOPS

THE CHARACTERS

ODYSSEUS, King of Ithaca
POLYPHEMUS, The Cyclops
SILENUS, leader of the Satyrs
CHORUS OF SATYRS
Sailors, following Odysseus

THE SCENE

Before the Cave of POLYPHEMUS, *near the seashore
on the slopes of Mount Etna in Sicily.*

THE CYCLOPS

In front of the Cave of POLYPHEMUS, *the Cyclops,
on the slopes of Mount Etna in Sicily.
Enter* SILENUS *carrying a rake.*

SILENUS:

Look, Dionysus, how both day and night,
In youth and age, I toil for your delight!
Remember how, when Hera's madness came,
We fled the Nymphs that nursed you; when the flame
Of Giant-War fell on us, how I stood
In the front rank beside you and made good
My claims to valour, hurling through the shield
Of great Enceladus this spear I wield ...
Er – used to wield ... No worthless comrade, I!
Sweet Bacchus, don't forget me! It's no lie,   10
You've got the trophies still of our Great War!

But now I suffer worse than all before:
Since Hera's had you kidnapped on the seas
By Tuscan pirates – *I* must, if you please,
Become a sailor and with my quaint boys
Set out to seek you. These transpontine ploys
Don't suit me, but I do them pretty well:
Step mast! Hoist sail! Come, plough the ocean swell
Leaning upon your oars, with splash and strain,
Whitening with foam the green and purple plain   20
Of the unharvested sea! Yes, that's the style
Of questing heroes ... So, for mile on mile
We sought you, master – till a sudden gale
Caught us near Cape Malea, filled each sail
With furious wind and desperate tempest shock,
Drove us to this most wild Etnean rock.
Here where the Sea-god's one-eyed children dwell
The Cyclopes, each in his rocky cell,

17

Man-eating monsters – here I am, a slave
30 To Polyphemus! I must clean his cave,
I, who have danced with Bacchus! Guard his flocks,
And with my sons toil up these beastly rocks
To tend the lambs and ewes. My job's to fill
The water casks, and scrape – it makes me ill –
The filthy floor after his nasty meals!
I, great Silenus! Just think how it feels
To rake up dung and litter from the floor,
To make all clean for one whom I abhor
Ere he comes home tonight and goes to sleep
40 Here in the cave among his silly sheep.

Hallo! I see my sons drive home the beasts
For our vile master … Hey! Here are no feasts
To glut you as of old! I'm sure your measures
In dance and song are ghosts of ancient pleasures
We knew in days gone by; sad heart recalls
When we brought Bacchus home to Althea's halls!

Enter CHORUS OF SATYRS, *driving the sheep of*
POLYPHEMUS.

CHORUS:
Son of a ram and a noble ewe,
Where on earth are you climbing to?
Does not the breeze blow softly here
50   Setting the grassy plains aquiver?
Troughs are put for you by the cave
  Filled with water sweet from the river;
Surely, surely all that you crave
Waits within for you? Swift! Draw near
Where your lambs are crying for you!

This way! This way, mother of lambs,
  Feed on the grass nearby!
Move on! Move on! toughest of rams,
  Or I'll teach you the reason why!

For I'll take this stone from the Cyclops' door   60
And bruise you, batter you, make you sore!

Udders ready! Each milk-full ewe!
Here be lambs demanding their due!
Your little ones who have slept all day
  Miss you now, you can hear them bleating!
Here they wait for you in the fold;
  Leave the meadows, have done with eating,
Seek the cave, for the hills grow cold,
But Etna's warm if you come this way
Where your lambs are crying for you!   70

Move on! Move on! toughest of rams,
  Feed on the grass nearby!
This way! This way! mother of lambs,
  Or I'll teach you the reason why!
For I'll take this stone from the Cyclops' door
And bruise you, batter you, make you sore!

    Alas, no Dionysus here,
      No dancing company,
    Nor Bacchic revellers appear,
      No cymbals clashing   80
      By waters dashing,
    No fresh wine poured for me!

    Not with the Nymphs on Nysa now
      'Iacchus!' rings our cry:
    Nor with fleet Maenads 'neath the bough
      Queen Love pursuing –
      Up and doing! –
    Where the white Bacchants fly.

      Iacchus! Iacchus!
      Oh dear lord Bacchus,   90
    Where go you now alone,

With gold hair flying?
While we are dying
In caverns dry as stone!

And I, your follower,
Good wine-swallower,
Languish, the Cyclops' thrall;
In goatskin coated
Am I, who doted
100   On you: oh hear our call!

SILENUS:

Be silent, sons, and bid the lesser slaves
Gather the flocks and pen them in the caves.

A SATYR:

Done! But what's happened, father? Let us know!

SILENUS:

Close to the coast I see a Grecian prow:
The rowers, with some man of note, are now
Nearing this cave. By bag and water-flask
I guess that they have landed here to ask
For fresh provisions. Oh the wretched men!
Whence come they that they do not know the den
110 Of Polyphemus with the man-trap jaw,
Who eats his visitors, and asks for more!
     Be silent: now I'll ask them, that I will,
Why they would visit Etna's fatal hill.

Enter ODYSSEUS *and his followers, carrying baskets
and water-vessels.*

ODYSSEUS:

Friends, can you show me some fresh water spring
To remedy our thirst? And can you bring
Food for poor starving sailors in their need? ...
But what is this? Can we have come indeed

To Dionysus' home? Do I not see
A band of Satyrs sporting on the lea?
First let me greet their leader: Hail, my friend!   120

SILENUS:
　Hail stranger! Say – who, and from whence, you wend.

ODYSSEUS:
　Ithaca's lord, Odysseus is my name.

SILENUS:
　Sisyphus' kin, a quibbler – known to fame!

ODYSSEUS:
　Yes. But you need not try your cheek on me!

SILENUS:
　Hmm … Tell us whence you come to Sicily?

ODYSSEUS:
　From Ilion, we – straight from the Trojan War.

SILENUS:
　Why did you not land on your native shore?

ODYSSEUS:
　Strong tempests forced me here across the sea.

SILENUS:
　Exactly the mishap that troubled me.

ODYSSEUS:
　Oh; but how did bad weather chance to bring … ?   130

SILENUS:
　Us? We chased pirates who had seized our king.

ODYSSEUS:
　What land is this? What natives may I seek?

SILENUS:
　Sicily. And there towers great Etna's peak.

ODYSSEUS:
　And are there castles, towns, or hamlets, then?

SILENUS:

Not one. These bare rocks are devoid of men.

ODYSSEUS:

And who dwells here? Just the wild beasts alone?

SILENUS:

The Cyclopes, in caves and walls of stone.

ODYSSEUS:

Who rules them, or is this a social state?

SILENUS:

A commune: no one's either low or great.

ODYSSEUS:

140   How do they live then? Do they reap and thresh?

SILENUS:

Mostly on cheese; they'll kill a sheep for flesh.

ODYSSEUS:

And wine of Bacchus here is highly prized?

SILENUS:

There's not a drop: they're quite uncivilized!

ODYSSEUS:

And are they just to strangers? Are they kind?

SILENUS:

If strangers leave themselves as food behind!

ODYSSEUS:

God! It's not human flesh on which they sup?

SILENUS:

Whoever comes is simply eaten up.

ODYSSEUS:

The Cyclops … Where's he? … Not at home, I hope?

SILENUS:

Out hunting with his dogs on Etna's slope.

ODYSSEUS:

150   You know what you must do to help us now?

SILENUS:

I don't: but what we can we will, I vow.

ODYSSEUS:

Supply our grievous want, food fit to eat.

SILENUS:

There's nothing here worth tasting ... (ODYSSEUS *looks threateningly*) Well, there's meat –

ODYSSEUS:

A splendid cure for hunger; if you please –

SILENUS:

Then there's cow's milk, and lots of curdled cheese.

ODYSSEUS:

Show me: we'll make a bargain here, I think.

SILENUS:

Well, it depends on how you're off for chink.

ODYSSEUS:

Hang money. I've the Bacchic juice instead.

SILENUS:

My darling wine? What a sweet word you've said!

ODYSSEUS:

Old Maron's gift ... divine, or I'm beguiled ...   160

SILENUS:

What, Maron, whom I dandled as a child?

ODYSSEUS (*nodding*):

Son of that god who gave mankind the vine.

SILENUS:

Where is it? Here or in your ship, this wine?

ODYSSEUS:

Here in the skin, old fellow. Don't you see?

SILENUS:

That? Scarcely an aperitif for me!

ODYSSEUS:

Nonsense: two draughts at least, even for you.

SILENUS:
Wine, the world's sweetest fountain ... Hurry, do!

ODYSSEUS:
Unmingled wine would floor you when you're dry!

SILENUS:
A sample tempts a purchaser to buy!

ODYSSEUS:
170   Well, I've a cup besides this bulging skin.

SILENUS:
Refresh my memory – quick, pour it in!

ODYSSEUS (*pouring wine*):
Watch!

SILENUS:
　　　Yummy-yum! Oh what a heavenly smell!

ODYSSEUS:
You see?

SILENUS:
　　　No, but, by Zeus, my nose can tell!

ODYSSEUS:
Taste it! Deeds before words in such employ!

SILENUS:
Yum! Yum! Great Bacchus, I could dance with joy!
Ooo! Ah! (*He drinks with noisy appreciation.*)

ODYSSEUS:
Hmmm ... Did the wine flow sweetly past your lips?

SILENUS:
It tingled to my very finger tips!

ODYSSEUS:
I've golden coin as well, if you aspire –

SILENUS:
180   Confound your gold! Wine's all that I require!

ODYSSEUS:

Good. Then bring cheeses now: and goat's flesh too.

SILENUS:

I'll risk it, and not care what *he* can do.
Yes, for one cup of wine I'll bring you now
The Cyclopean flocks from Etna's brow!
Oh to be really drunk! Why, then I'd leap
From the Leucadian cliff into the deep:
I'd shut my eyes and dive! The man is mad
Who won't get drunk when drink is to be had.
If I were drunk – God, how I'd chase the girls!
One just forgets all else when dancing whirls   190
The drink about one's wits! I'd catch them, too!
And then ... Well, well, we know what I would do ...
There's no one here to kiss – except the wine,
And that I'm off to earn. I'll make it mine!
I'll rob the Cyclops, make the monster cry
Hot tears from out that glaring central eye.

SILENUS *goes into the cave.*

A SATYR:

Well now, Odysseus, for a friendly chat.

ODYSSEUS:

As friend to friend, then, what would you be at?

SATYR:

Did you burn Troy? Did you get Helen back?

ODYSSEUS:

We did indeed put Priam's town to sack!   200

SATYR:

Oh-ho! And did you all share Helen then?
I know she loves a multitude of men!
Why, first the greasy Paris charmed her sight
With his outlandish clothes; it wasn't right

25

To leave good Menelaus, and the kid,
And bolt with Paris. Well, I never did!
Zeus ought to ban all women utterly ...
Except, of course, some jolly girls for me!

Re-enter SILENUS *laden with food.*

SILENUS:

Look, King Odysseus, mutton, goats' flesh, cheese!
210 Come, fill your bags as tight as you can squeeze,
Then get you gone as quickly as you may.
But don't forget my wine, that heavenly pay
You promised me ...
My God! Too late indeed!
I see the Cyclops coming at full speed!

ODYSSEUS:

Quick, quick, old man! Which way ought we to fly?

SILENUS:

Into the cave! Run! Find a place to lie ...

ODYSSEUS:

That's madness – running straight into the net!

SILENUS:

The cave is full of holes, he may forget ...

ODYSSEUS:

What am I saying? I'd disgrace my name,
220 Fleeing one man! Yes Troy would share the shame!
How many times have I with mighty shield,
To twice five thousand Trojans scorned to yield!
If death is here, then bravely die I will:
If life, my fame will then show brighter still!

SILENUS *has stolen away into the cave. Now*
POLYPHEMUS *enters, and speaks to the* SATYRS.

POLYPHEMUS:

What's all this slacking? Hurry on there, do!
And stop that noise! Here is no Bacchus, who

Delights in tympanies, and cymbals' clashings!
Is the new cheese stored well, with good, sound lashings?
And what about my precious sheep? The lambs
I hope are feeding quietly from their dams?   230
Speak, or I'll take and beat you till you roar!
Look up! Why are you gazing on the floor?

THE SATYRS (*looking quickly at the sky*):
Up? Why, we're looking Zeus between the eyes:
We're seeing stars! We're gazing at the skies!

POLYPHEMUS:
Then have you got my dinner well prepared?

SATYRS:
Why yes, it's waiting – if your gullet's aired!

POLYPHEMUS:
And is my milk quite ready in the cup?

SATYRS:
Ready? Why, you could drink a tub-full up!

POLYPHEMUS:
Ewe's milk or cow's milk; or the two in one?

SATYRS:
Both – either – You'll drink *us* before you're done!   240

POLYPHEMUS:
Not on your life! You'd give me belly-ache;
You'd kick my throat and all my paunch would quake!
    (*He suddenly notices* ODYSSEUS *and the sailors.*)
Hallo! Hallo! Who are those people there?
Outlaws or thieves? And did they really dare
To lead away my sheep and steal my cheese?
But here's my slave … What shameful marks are these?

SILENUS (*entering with blood and dirt on face and head*):
Alas, I'm beaten till I'm nearly dead.

POLYPHEMUS:
By whom? Whose finger prints are on your head?

SILENUS:

These thieves, my lord, to rob you did conspire.

POLYPHEMUS:

250 Rob me? A god – who had a god for sire!

SILENUS:

I told them so – they didn't care a damn!
They ate your cheese, and robbed you lamb by lamb;
Moreover they declared they'd hang you high
And pluck your guts out through your single eye;
From your great frame the skin they meant to flay
And use your bones as ballast. Or convey
Yourself to slavery, securely bound,
To carry stones, or twirl a mill-wheel round.

POLYPHEMUS:

Did they indeed? ... Get busy then, I say!
260 Sharpen my carving knife, without delay!
Stack high my hearth with faggots; light the fire!
I'll have the very supper I desire.
I'm sick of eating vermin; lions and deer
Grow boring. But tonight there's better cheer:
Fat steak of man, grilled to a lovely brown,
Or human stew – with soup to help it down!
My mouth is simply watering for man!

SILENUS:

You're right, a change of diet is just the plan;
And really it's a longish time, my lord,
270 Since the last strangers stopped to grace your board!

ODYSSEUS (*in a panic*):

Cyclops! A moment! We are guests indeed,
We came for food – we did not come to feed!
This villain sold me, for a cup of wine,
These lambs and cheeses – which, it seems, were thine –
I knew thee not, nor recked thou wast divine ...
Listen! ... It was a bargain, sheep for wine!

And now he's telling you a bloody lie
Because you've caught him stealing on the sly!

SILENUS:
Me? Devil take him if – –

ODYSSEUS (*interrupting*):
                    I speak not true!

SILENUS:
Good Polyphemus here I swear to you   280
By great Poseidon – I would never trip so!
I swear by Triton, Nereus, by Calypso;
By all the Nereids and the finny fish –
Or anyone aquatic that you wish –
I didn't give a single thing away.
Dear, sweet, good-looking Cyclops – listen, pray!
If I'm a thief let all my sons be hurled
To Hell! My sons – my one joy in this world!

A SATYR:
Hold hard! Hold hard! He gave the things away
Quite freely to these strangers. And I say   290
That if I'm lying, let *him* go below …
One must be fair to strangers, as you know!

POLYPHEMUS:
It's you who lie! I'd trust him anywhere:
Not Rhadamanthys is more just and fair.
But tell me, strangers, from what land you come,
What place you seek, what city is your home?

ODYSSEUS (*cautiously*):
We're Ithacans by race, from conquered Troy
We sail, but suffer from the sea's annoy
Which drives us, noble Cyclops, to your land.

POLYPHEMUS:
What, have you fought on the Scamandrian strand   300
For the false Helen, that unenvied spoil?

ODYSSEUS:

  We have indeed endured that lengthy toil.

POLYPHEMUS:

  A rotten business. For one worthless whore
  The flower of Greece sought out the Phrygian shore?

ODYSSEUS:

  Do not blame Helen; all that she has done
  Was by a god's design. But you, great son
  Of the earth-shaking lord, we beg you now
  Be merciful to us. You must allow
  That we who visit you are friends indeed.
310 Think: and control your truly impious greed.
  Many a temple on Hellenic soil
  Reared to your father's honour with hard toil
  Bears out my claim: on the Taenarian strand
  Sacred, inviolate; and rising grand
  Above Malea; lovely as a dream
  On Sunium's height the fretted columns gleam,
  Guarded by great Athena; and the peace
  Of quiet Geraestus. All the land of Greece
  Proves what I say – the land we have kept free
320 From Phrygian conquest and profanity.
  Hellas, your father, and yourself as well
  Have common cause with us; for you too dwell,
  Here in the shade of Etna's fiery jaws,
  Upon the fringe of Hellas and her laws.

    Then, as a Hellene, hear the suppliant's prayer:
  Receive us, your sea-guests, with presents fair,
  With food and clothes and comfort. Far more fit
  Is such a welcome, than with ghoulish spit
  To pierce our limbs and glut your appetite.
330   Enough of Greeks have known death's awful night
  In Priam's land: too many widows weep
  The cruel spear-harvest rotting heap on heap;

Old fathers and grey-headed mothers wail
Their childless age. Oh, do not swell the tale
Of slaughtered Greeks; forswear your hellish roast,
Forswear it, and be rather the good host
Who welcomes men in kindliness. Forgo
This carnal lust; it well may work you woe.

SILENUS:

Cyclops! Be warned! He's selling you a pup!
Swallow him whole! Eat every morsel up!   340
And don't forget his tongue! That ought to be
The medicine to promote loquacity!

POLYPHEMUS:

Midget, the really wise man's god is gain:
All else is mere pretence, vaunting and vain.
What of each sea-girt pile and sanctuary?
My father's temples are no use to me.
I scorn the bolt of Zeus you call divine!
How do I know his power is more than mine?
That's all that counts. And when the rain comes down
I've got my snug, dry cave, in which I drown   350
The thunder with loud belches, feasting there
On some roast game, or veal, and banish care
With gurgling vats of milk. And when the snow
Comes from the bitter north, why then I blow
The embers to a blaze, throw on a tree,
Don a warm fur – and what's the snow to me!
The earth bears grass, whether it will or not,
To feed my flocks and herds. So tell me what
I need with sacrifice – which none deserve?
My belly is the only god I serve!   360
It's simple sense that man's first care should be
To please himself: no other deity
Is half so pleasing as a well-fed man.
    As for the fool who forms himself a plan,

31

A code of rules to make him sick and sad,
I wish him joy of it, and think he's mad.
I've got more sense than to deny myself!
So to the pot you go: nor prayers nor pelf
Shall save you. Here's true hospitality:
370   A warm place in my – belly – presently!
   Come in! The cauldron waits, the water boils:
My welcome frees a man from all his toils!

ODYSSEUS:

Alas! Have I escaped the Trojan spear,
Have I escaped the sea, to perish here
According to this monster's barbarous use?
   Oh Pallas! Oh thou goddess, born of Zeus,
Now, now assist me! Dangers greater far
Are these than any in the Trojan War.
And thou who sittest on the throne most high,
380   Look down, oh Zeus, from out the starry sky!
For if this impious outrage should befall,
Thou art not Zeus, nor any god at all!

POLYPHEMUS *now drives* ODYSSEUS *and his sailors
into the cave.*

CHORUS:

   Cyclops, Cyclops, open your lips,
     Get ready your gaping throat!
Down each collop-of-stranger slips,
     Boiled or roasted,
     Fried or toasted,
As you sit in your cave and gloat:
     Dress them, draw them,
390   Chew them and gnaw them,
Served on the skin of a goat!

We don't want to share your dinner,
   For your belly that suffices!
Cram it full, you fat old sinner,
   With your impious sacrifices.

Cyclops, those who gobble strangers
Risk a multitude of dangers.

Pitiless, merciless you who stuff
   Suppliants down your throat,
Snatched from your hearthstone, tender or tough;   400
     Gashing and gutting,
     Biting and cutting
The food on which you dote;
     Roasting men speedily,
     Eating them greedily,
Served on the skin of a goat!

We don't want to share your dinner,
   For your belly that suffices!
Cram it full, you fat old sinner,
   With your impious sacrifices.   410
Cyclops, those who gobble strangers
Risk a multitude of dangers!

  Cries are heard from the cave, and ODYSSEUS *rushes out.*

ODYSSEUS (*inarticulately*):
  Oh Zeus, what shall I say? What have I seen?
  Things past all words, and yet these things have been!

A SATYR:
  Whatever's up, Odysseus? Oh, did you
  See your friends being eaten? Tell me, do!

ODYSSEUS:
  Why yes. He felt us all, and then and there
  He chose the fattest and the fleshiest pair ...

SATYRS:
  How? You poor fellow! ... Tell us all you saw.

ODYSSEUS:
  He lit a great fire on the rocky floor   420
  The moment we were in, and heaped it high
  With waggon-loads of oak logs nicely dry.

And then he spread his couch beside the fire
Of pine fronds. Next he turned him to the byre
And milked his cows, filling a mighty pot
Which held at least three gallons; and he got
His goblet ready – several feet across
It was, and very deep. Pausing to toss
A heap of skewers ready to his hand,
430 He filled a cauldron which he set to stand
And boil upon the fire: but all my gaze
Was held by those vile skewers, for the blaze
Showed the cruel points he sharpened with the blade
Of his great pruning hook. And more dismayed
I was to see wide dripping-pans set out
To catch the bloody gravy gout by gout.
Worse followed, for when once this cook of Hell
Had put all ready, then – I weep to tell
What chanced to my poor friends, such unconcern
440 The Cyclops showed as he with one quick turn
Flung one against the cauldron and then caught
The second by his ankle and cut short
His life by braining him against the point
Of a hard rock; then dressed and set the joint
To roast before the fire. His other dish
He chopped and stewed and seasoned to his wish.
    Oh then the tears came pouring from my eyes,
What could I bring but pity for their cries?
I had to help the Cyclops as he bade.
450   Meanwhile my comrades, very much afraid,
Cowered like birds, striving to hide from sight,
Their faces pale and bloodless with pure fright.
    When he was gorged as full as he could squeeze,
He gave a stinking belch, and lay at ease
Digesting my poor friends. Then by the grace
Of some kind god a cunning thought found place

In my distracted mind: straightway I poured
A cup of Maron's wine and said: 'My lord,
Great Cyclops, thou who art indeed the son
Of god Poseidon, see what liquors run   460
'Twixt Grecian lips; what ecstasy the vine
Yields by great Dionysus' will divine.'

   Then he, made thirsty by his loathsome meal,
Took it and gulped it down, and seemed to feel
Some touch of kindness, for he said: 'Dear guest,
After sweet food, sweet drinks are always best!'
And seeing that it pleased him, I filled up
With un-mixed wine another brimming cup,
Knowing full well that drink would take its toll
Of his weak wits. He swallowed bowl on bowl,   470
Seeking the moment's pleasure. Before long
Well warmed with wine he burst into a song,
A base accompaniment to the shrill cries
Of my despairing men. Then it seemed wise
For me to slip away and plot with you
How to escape: I felt that Satyrs too
Must long for freedom, long again to dwell
Among the Naiad Nymphs they love so well,
And walk with Dionysus as of old.

   Your father's on my side, but though made bold   480
With Bacchic juice, that's made his legs unsteady!
He's on his back in there, the wine's so heady
It's tripped him up. But you are young and strong:
So let's plan our escape; then, before long
With your dear Dionysus you will be;
The Cyclops can't compare with such as he!

CHORUS:

   Oh dearest friend! Could we but see the day
Of freedom dawn at last and get away
For ever from the Cyclops! Far too long
Has he deprived us of both drink and song!   490

ODYSSEUS:
Listen then to the punishment in store
For him, which makes our safety quite secure.

CHORUS (*ecstatically*):
Sweeter than is the Asian lyre's strain
Would be the voice that told of Cyclops slain!

ODYSSEUS:
Sozzled with drink, he plans to go and cheer
His brother Cyclopes who live quite near.

CHORUS:
Oh ... So you mean to catch him when alone,
Or push him from some overhanging stone.

ODYSSEUS:
No, no, I much prefer some subtler wile!

CHORUS:
500   What then? We know you're famous for your guile.

ODYSSEUS:
I'll make him change his plans; point out that sharing
Will only make him short, that if he's sparing,
The precious drink will last a longer time
And make his own enjoyment more sublime.
He'll take the hint and drink, and before long
He'll fall asleep because the wine's so strong.
    I've found an olive stake deep in the cave:
One end of it with my good sword I'll shave
Into a point; and in the fire ignite
510   The sharpened part. Then, when it's well alight
I'll use it on the Cyclops' single eye
And bore it out with fire. For you and I
Will spin it like the drill that ship-wrights turn
With double thongs. In this way we will burn
The monster's single eye and blind him quite.

CHORUS:
Hurrah! We're simply crazy with delight!

ODYSSEUS:

   And then, my friends, we'll load the ships and you
   And old Silenus shall complete my crew
   And sail away full speed from this vile land.

CHORUS:

   Come, let us help you with the burning brand: 520
   Let's use it as a sacrificial knife;
   We'd like to share in shortening *his* life!

ODYSSEUS:

   You may: the brand is far too big for me.

CHORUS:

   A hundred waggon-loads would seem to be
   The weight of one, if, like a wasps'-nest, we
   Could scoop his loathsome eye out speedily!

ODYSSEUS:

   Then silence now: you know the plan, and when
   I call, do as I bid you. In his den
   My friends are still unsaved, and I'll not fly,
   As well I might, and leave them there to die.   530
   It were a coward's trick to run away,
   Deserting them to be an ogre's prey!

CHORUS:

   Say who first and say who second
     Now will spin the burning brand
   Through his eyelid; though it lie hid
     Cyclops, you must understand
     We, to take your eye have planned –
   We, with whom you never reckoned!

   (*Sounds of shouting and drunken singing in the Cave.*)

   Hush a minute! There he goes
     With his music all discordant.   540
   Such a rumpus only shows
     We've good reason to be mordant!

Can we teach him time and rhythm?
Such instruction suits not with 'im!
We should make him, that is clear,
Blind in eye as blind of ear!

A SATYR (*singing*):
I sing as a lover
  Emboldened with wine,
Setting out to discover
550   Which lass will be mine!

Come drink, pretty sweeting
  Come drink with me deep
For kisses are fleeting
  And after comes sleep!

What lass am I bearing
  To bed at my side?
When a lover comes faring,
  Each door opens wide!

POLYPHEMUS *enters singing drunkenly*:
I sing as a glutton
560   Top-heavy with wine,
Full fed with man-mutton
  What pleasures are mine!

Oh drinking and eating
  They weigh me down deep,
But such cargoes are fleeting;
  Away let me leap

To see who'll be sharing
  These orgies of mine!
Quick, stranger, come bearing
570   Fresh bumpers of wine!

CHORUS:
    Hush a minute! Who is here
      With an eye so sweetly gleaming?

Now he leaves his single lair
   Like a lovely bride in seeming,
Come to greet her waiting lovers
Till her brow the garland covers ...
We'll crown your brow with colours fresh
Most lover-like, *and* pierce your flesh!

ODYSSEUS:
   Cyclops, attend! I'm expert in the lore
   Of Bacchus – whom you've lately seen me pour.   580

POLYPHEMUS (*speaking thickly*):
   This Bacchus: as a god, how's he defined?

ODYSSEUS:
   Giver of life's best joys to humankind.

POLYPHEMUS:
   I drank him, and he tasted very nice.

ODYSSEUS:
   This god requires no painful sacrifice!

POLYPHEMUS:
   And for a temple does he choose this skin?

ODYSSEUS:
   He's happy with whatever place he's in!

POLYPHEMUS:
   I don't think that true gods should have a skin.

ODYSSEUS:
   The outward look makes not the god within!

POLYPHEMUS:
   I hate the husk, the kernel tastes divine.

ODYSSEUS:
   Then taste again: drink, and be glad with wine.   590

POLYPHEMUS:
   Should I not stand a drink to my dear brothers?

ODYSSEUS:
   This rare communion would be spoilt by others.

POLYPHEMUS:
　It would be more fun drinking among friends.

ODYSSEUS:
　There'd be a riot: you know how such fun ends.

POLYPHEMUS:
　When I get drunk nobody dares be rude!

ODYSSEUS:
　Still, better to get drunk in solitude.

POLYPHEMUS:
　When drinking, one is wise to have a spree.

ODYSSEUS:
　But drunk at home, the wiser man is he!

POLYPHEMUS:
　What do you think, Silenus? If one stops ...

SILENUS (*with drunken gravity*):
600　Shtay! ... 'Nough's as good's a feast – my dear Cy-clops!

POLYPHEMUS (*sitting down suddenly*):
　Well, here's nice flowers and grass on which to sink.

SILENUS (*hiding the wine-cup*):
　An' sunshine ... Jus' the weather for a drink!
　Sit by me close: we make a pretty pair!

POLYPHEMUS:
　There now ...
　Hey! Why's the cup behind you? Do you dare ...

SILENUS:
　Cup? Oh, to keep it safe!

POLYPHEMUS:
　　　　　　　　　It isn't fair!
　Put it between us; let me guard my share!
　Thingamy! Stranger! What's your name? You there!

ODYSSEUS:
　Why, Nobody! ... Now, treat me as a friend.

POLYPHEMUS:

I will! I'll eat you at the very end!   610

ODYSSEUS:

Dear Cyclops, you are really very kind.

POLYPHEMUS (*to* SILENUS):

Hey! Stealing wine, you rogue! D'you think I'm blind?

SILENUS:

The dear wine longed to kiss my lovely lips ...

POLYPHEMUS:

Lovely? They'd turn it rotten in two sips!

SILENUS:

You used to call me pretty! 'Struth you did!

POLYPHEMUS:

Shut up! And fill the flagon as you're bid!

SILENUS:

How's that? I'd better try it, don't you think ...

POLYPHEMUS:

Give, curse you! Give!

SILENUS:

                I really ought to drink

Your noble health, and see you crowned with flowers!

POLYPHEMUS:

False steward!

SILENUS:

             No! But this sweet wine of ours   620

Is holy: wipe your mouth before you drink!

POLYPHEMUS:

There! Beard and whiskers are quite clean I think!

SILENUS:

Then hold it up like this ... So ... Do you follow?

Just as you see me (*he drinks it down*) – as you saw me

    swallow!

POLYPHEMUS:
Why, what the –?

SILENUS:
What a gorgeous gulp was that!

POLYPHEMUS:
Well, Nobody shall pour the rest, that's flat!

ODYSSEUS:
I'm an old hand with wine; it's used to me!

POLYPHEMUS:
Then hurry up!

ODYSSEUS (*pouring*):
There! Drink it silently.

POLYPHEMUS:
It's not so easy to keep quiet, I find.

ODYSSEUS:
630   Here, take the drink – and leave no drop behind.
(*Aside*) I wish blind-drunk made you both drunk and
    blind!

POLYPHEMUS (*gulping it down*):
Yum-yum! The vine's a wondrous plant indeed!

ODYSSEUS:
Swill plenty down after a mighty feed
And keep your throat well oiled – sleep like a top!
Bacchus will parch you if you leave a drop!

POLYPHEMUS (*very drunk now*):
Oooh! Ah!
I can't stand up! Oh, what a lovely feeling!
The earth's the earth ... nex' minute it's the ceiling!
I'm going up! I'll see the throne of Zeus
640   An' the whole pack of gods ... Not for my use,
No, I'd not kiss. The Graces can't seduce
Me from this lovely boy this Ganymede!
A fig for Graces! I've got all I need!

SILENUS:
Good God! Me Ganymede? I am undone!

POLYPHEMUS:
Like Zeus I'll grab you – Dardanus's son!

SILENUS:
I'm done for, boys! I'm in for something bad.

POLYPHEMUS:
Don't jilt a fellow 'cos he's drunken-mad!

SILENUS:
At last I see the vile effects of wine!

POLYPHEMUS *drags* SILENUS *into the Cave.*

ODYSSEUS:
Now, children of the god who rules the vine,
The time has come! The monster's sick with drink;   650
Or will be any moment; then he'll sink
In swinish slumber. I can smell the smoke
That rises from the brand made hot to poke
His single eye out. Quick, into the den,
And let me see you bear yourselves like men!

CHORUS:
      Our courage is as firm as any rock,
      As adamant indeed. No need to knock,
      But go right in, lest he should chance to wake.
      Hurry! And mind you're handy with that stake!

ODYSSEUS (*praying*):
Hephaestus, King of Etna, aid me now   660
To burn the eye beneath this monster's brow!
And, child of gloomy Night, Immortal Sleep
Plunge this god-hated beast in slumber deep.
Let not my Odyssey be broken short,
Nor suffer heroes who at Troy have fought
To stuff this monster's gizzard – one who fears
No god or mortal. Else thy strength appears

No strength divine, and I must deem, though loath,
That Chance alone rules gods and mortals both!

ODYSSEUS *goes into the Cave, but the* SATYRS *hang
back and sing.*

CHORUS:

670   Get ready!
               Go steady!
          The torture is ripe
This eater of guests by the throttle to gripe!
               Get ready!
              Hold steady
         The fire which is nigh
To burn into ashes his fire-bearing eye!

         In cinders well hidden
           The olive shoot lies;
680   Now drink as you're bidden –
          Drink, close up his eyes!

        Drink, Cyclops, in sorrow,
          Who soon will be blind!
        We'll sail on the morrow
          And leave you behind!

          Then Bacchus
          Won't lack us
        Who long to behold
The garland of ivy his bright locks enfold.
690   No, Bacchus
          Won't lack us,
        But Cyclops, grown sad
Alone in his desert – and won't we be glad!

ODYSSEUS (*coming angrily out of the Cave*):
Shut up, you fools! ... Have you gone mad? Don't dare
Even to breathe. Be tongue-tied; yes, take care

44

That you don't cough; don't even dare to blink
In case you wake the monster on the brink
Of our red-hot assault upon his eye.

SATYRS:

Silent? We'll eat the air! ... At least we'll try!

ODYSSEUS:

Come then and help; the weapon's burning bright;   700
Just what we need to quench an ogre's sight!

A SATYR (*indicating his companions*):

Well, choose which Satyr first should hold the brand
Destined to blind the Cyclops. Here we stand
All waiting anxiously to lend a hand.

ANOTHER SATYR (*hastily separating himself*):

I'm much too distant here, of course, to try
And reach into the cave and burn his eye!

ANOTHER SATYR:

How odd! I've got the cramp – can't move for pain ...

ANOTHER SATYR:

That's just my case! Somehow I've chanced to sprain
My ankle ... Bound to happen, standing here!

ODYSSEUS:

What, sprained it standing still?

ANOTHER SATYR:

                        It's very queer,   710
But I've got ashes in my eyes – or dust.

ODYSSEUS:

Afraid to help? ... You fill me with disgust.

ANOTHER SATYR:

Well really, you can't say that we're afraid!
In care of self true courage is displayed –
I'd be a fool to risk jaw, leg, or arm!
And anyhow, I know an Orphic charm

Will pierce that great eye with the burning pole –
And blind the Cyclops by remote control!

ODYSSEUS:

I've always heard you Satyrs were the end,
720   And now I know it's true! Well, I've a friend
Or two among my comrades who will help.
Stay here, you cowards, but see to it: don't yelp
Before you're hurt. Speak words of courage; sing
Some stirring tune: loud let the glad notes ring!

SATYRS:

Fear? We don't know its meaning! Fierce and strong
We'll blind that dreadful Cyclops with our song!

ODYSSEUS *goes into the Cave and the* SATYRS *gather
round expectantly.*

CHORUS:

> Ha! Ha! Hasten the thrust
> > Most noble of men
> > In the maneater's den!
730   Burn into dust,
> His eye; then we trust
> > He'll not see us again!

> Ha! Ha! Kindle the brand,
> > Twist it about,
> > Thrust in and out!
> Take care where you stand!
> Beware of his hand!
> > He'll be desperate, no doubt!

POLYPHEMUS, *roaring with rage, appears at the Cave mouth
with his hands to his forehead.*

POLYPHEMUS:

My eye's all shrivelled up! I rub in vain!

A SATYR:

740   What a sweet song! Come, sing it us again!

POLYPHEMUS (*turning to the Cave*):
Woe's me! Alas! I'm blinded! Oh my eye!
But you, you wretched mice, don't think to fly!
There's no escape, I've got you in my trap:
I'm ready if you bolt, with hands to clap
Upon you as you pass; and then, one snap!

A SATYR:
Cyclops, what's all the row?

POLYPHEMUS:
                              Oh, I'm destroyed!

A SATYR:
And also very wicked!

POLYPHEMUS:
                         And annoyed!

A SATYR:
Did you get drunk and fall into the flame?

POLYPHEMUS:
Nobody stabbed –

SATYRS:
                   Then nobody's to blame!

POLYPHEMUS:
Nobody blinded me!

SATYRS:
                     Then you're not blind!   750

POLYPHEMUS:
I wish you'd suffered –

SATYRS:
                        Nothing? We'd not mind!

POLYPHEMUS:
Don't joke and play the fool. Where's Nobody?

SATYRS:
Nowhere, and everywhere! Where should he be?

POLYPHEMUS:

The stranger – gave me wine and made me drunk –
And then he blinded me – the dirty skunk!

A SATYR:

It's rash, you know, to swallow so much wine!

POLYPHEMUS:

I've got the villains in this cave of mine!

ODYSSEUS *and his followers escape from the Cave as the*
SATYRS *delude* POLYPHEMUS, *who rushes from side to
side, tripping up, bumping his head, and so on. The effect
should be farcical and not tragic.*

A SATYR:

Why, so you have! They're hiding, mad with fear,
Close to the door.

POLYPHEMUS:

          I'll feel. Which hand is near?

A SATYR:

Your right hand.

POLYPHEMUS:

       Where?

A SATYR:

            You've got them! Near the
760   rock!

POLYPHEMUS:

Ow! Damn! I've caught my head an awful knock!

SATYRS:

They're getting out!

POLYPHEMUS:

         Not where you said they were.

SATYRS:

No, not *that* side!

POLYPHEMUS:

     Which side?

A SATYR:

Why, over here!

POLYPHEMUS:

You're mocking me! Don't cheat me when I'm ill!

SATYRS:

He's there! He's there! The man you want to kill!

POLYPHEMUS:

Where is that devil?

ODYSSEUS:

If it's me you mean,
Odysseus, here I am, safe and serene.

POLYPHEMUS (*stopping suddenly*):

What's that? What's that? What new name did you say?

ODYSSEUS:

My father named me on my natal day
Odysseus: you must look for vengeance when   770
You take to making impious meals of men.
Ill had I done, who shook the Trojan plain,
And sought not vengeance for my comrades slain!

POLYPHEMUS:

Alas, the oracle foretold it right:
Which said that you would rob me of my sight
Returning home from Troy ... It also told
Of punishment for being overbold;
How, for your cruel deed in blinding me,
For long you'd wander homeless on the sea.

ODYSSEUS:

I bid you weep! I have done what you say!   780
Think of us sailing on our homeward way
Leaving your land of Sicily behind.

POLYPHEMUS:

I may prevent it still, although I'm blind!
I know another path down to the beach
Which I can find by groping. If I reach

49

The place in time, I'll see if showers of stones
Can sink your ship, and break your hateful bones!

POLYPHEMUS goes blundering away on one side.

ODYSSEUS restrains the SATYRS, *silencing them and marshalling them in dumb show –* SILENUS, *still rather drunk, imitating his actions with ludicrous self-importance. When* POLYPHEMUS *is well out of sight,* ODYSSEUS *gives the signal, and sets off in the other direction, followed by his sailors, the* SATYRS, *and last of all* SILENUS, *fighting an imaginary rear-guard action. As they go, the* SATYRS *break into song,* SILENUS *trying in vain to restrain them.*

CHORUS:

> Hip, hip, hurray!
> We're on our way
790   As ship-mates of the Ithacan!
> And happy days
> We'll pass in praise
> Extolling Bacchus with a can!

Exeunt

NOTES TO *The Cyclops*

No definite date has been suggested for *The Cyclops*, though it is thought to be the earliest of the extant plays of Euripides, with a date before 440 B.C., which would probably place it earlier than *The Ichneutai* of Sophocles, in spite of its less formal style and manner.

While the story of Odysseus and Polyphemus is taken straight from Book IX of *The Odyssey*, Euripides has adapted his original to suit the requirements both of the stage and of the Satyric Drama. Homer makes no mention of Silenus and the Satyrs; and Euripides shortens the stay of Odysseus in the cave, allows only two sailors to be eaten, and omits the escape by means of the sheep just as he omits the other Cyclopes.

Line 1. Dionysus, the god of wine, was the son of Zeus and the mortal woman Semele. Hera, the wife of Zeus, persecuted him during his earthly existence as she did so many of her divine husband's mortal children. To keep him from her attention Zeus entrusted the child to the Nymphs of Mount Nysa in Asia Minor; but he did not escape her persecutions for long. According to an obscure myth, Dionysus was finally killed by the hero Perseus (Hera's representative, since he was king of her special country, Argos); he descended into the realm of Hades, where he rescued the spirit of his dead mother, and was later raised to Olympus and became one of the Gods.

He is also called Bacchus and Bromius, while he was frequently saluted with the cry 'Iacchus! Iacchus!'

Line 5. When war broke out between the Gods and the Giants (see note to *The Searching Satyrs*, line 462), some authorities say that Dionysus struck down the Giant called Enceladus; though the more usual story credits his overthrow to Pallas Athena, who flung upon him the mass of rock which became the island of Sicily. As he was not dead, his fiery breath continued to escape through Mount Etna.

Line 13, etc. The kidnapping of Dionysus by the Etruscan Pirates is the theme of the Homeric Hymn to that god.

Line 24. Cape Malea is the most southerly promontory of Greece.

Line 27, etc. Only the Cyclopes of Sicily seem to have been the children of Poseidon, god of the sea (their mother was the nymph Thoösa). Their far more terrible cousins, the Titan sons of Sky and Earth, were cast into Tartarus, or Hell, by conquering Zeus.

Line 46. The reference to Althea is obscure: no detailed account of this myth has come down to us. She was the wife of King Oeneus of Calydon, and mother of Meleager and of Deianira, last wife of Heracles. According to Apollodorus the mythographer some authorities make Ares the father of Meleager; and Dionysus the father of Deianira. Nonnos knew the legend also, but merely refers to Althea as one of his hero's past conquests. (*Dionysiaca* XLVIII. 555.)

Line 85, etc. Maenads or Bacchai ('Bacchanals' or 'Bacchants' are the most usual English literary forms) were the female followers of Dionysus, the temporarily frenzied women such as appear in Euripides' *Bacchae*.

Line 123. Sisyphus, the typical 'crafty lad' who in earlier writers was punished in Tartarus by rolling a stone to the top of a hill, whence it always returned to the bottom. Some writers called him, vaguely, the father of Odysseus: naturally the three craftiest men of antiquity, Sisyphus, Autolycus, and Odysseus, were assumed to be closely related.

Line 160. Maron, grandson of Dionysus and Ariadne, was priest of Apollo in Thrace. Odysseus spared him when he sacked the city of Ismarus, and in gratitude Maron gave him a skin of strong wine. (*Odyssey* IX.)

Line 168. Ancient Greek wine was so strong that it was customary to dilute it with water.

Line 186. The Leucadian cliff was a famous promontory on the island of Leucas, off the west coast of Greece.

Line 199. Helen of Sparta deserted her daughter Hermione and her husband, King Menelaus, and fled to Troy with Paris, son of its king Priam. She was much married, having already been carried off as a girl by Theseus, and marrying Deiphobus, another son of Priam, when Paris was killed. The Satyr voices the vulgar opinion of Helen;

at line 305 Odysseus defends her as the innocent victim of divine purposes.

Line 282. Triton was a minor marine deity, son of Poseidon; Nereus, father of the Nereids or sea-nymphs, an older sea-deity, was the son of Earth and Sea. Calypso in the *Odyssey* was the daughter of Atlas, but later writers gave her father as Ocean or Nereus.

Line 294. Rhadamanthys, son of Zeus and Europa, and brother of Minos, King of Crete, was so famous in his lifetime for his justice and legal wisdom that he was made one of the Judges of the Dead.

Line 300. Scamander was one of the rivers which flow through the plain of Troy.

Line 313, etc. Taenarum and Malea are capes at the south of Greece, while Sunium is the south cape of Attica, near Athens, and Geraestus, in Euboea, is the next promontory to the north.

Line 641. The Graces were the daughters of Zeus; they symbolized grace and beauty.

Line 642. Ganymede, son of King Dardanus of Troy, was a beautiful boy whom Zeus, in the form of an eagle, carried off to Olympus to be his cup-bearer.

Line 716. Orpheus was said to charm stones and trees into following him as he played on his lyre.

THE SEARCHING SATYRS

_____ • _____

THE CHARACTERS

The God PHOEBUS APOLLO

The God HERMES, son of Zeus and the nymph
    Maia

KYLLENE, nymph of the mountain so called

SILENUS, leader of the Satyrs

CHORUS OF SATYRS

THE SCENE

Before the Cave of Maia on the slopes of Mount Kyllene,
    a hill in Arcadia, in the North of the Peloponnese.

THE SEARCHING SATYRS

In front of the Cave of the Nymph KYLLENE *on the mountain
of the same name in Arcadia in southern Greece.
Enter* APOLLO *full of noble rage and grief – which
occasionally degenerates into petulance.*

APOLLO:

I am Apollo! Hearken, all below
To what a god proclaims! For you must know,
And gods above, what great Apollo vows:
A rich reward to him who finds my cows!
My heart is racked with pain: I've lost them all!
There's not one single heifer in my stall,
Nor cow, nor smallest calf. Where they can be
Is more than this all-seeing god can see!
I really did not think that god or man
Would dare such treason, such a stealthy plan   10
To steal my cattle and not leave a trace!

   I have been hurrying from place to place
Since first I heard the news, and I proclaim
My loss to gods and men. All are to blame,
And here I give them warning clear and fair,
Those who pretend that they are unaware
That I have lost my cows: they tempt their fate
Who would deceive me – and I do not prate!
For I'm Apollo, I would have you know.

   Where in the world did my poor cattle go?   20
I've visited so many tribes of men:
I've been to Libya, and come back again,
I've been as far as Troy, and gone across
Into Epirus – always at a loss.
And now I've come from Thrace, and on the way
Touched at Euboea, glanced round Sunium bay,

Visited Athens, been to Thebes as well,
Roamed on Parnassus where the Muses dwell,
Called at my shrine in Delphi, just in case
30 The cows came home to their accustomed place;
But no one there had seen them, so I came
To Corinth, but my luck was just the same.
Now I come straight from Argos to the land
Of fair Arcadia. Here great mountains stand
Across my way, and first Kyllene rears
Its lofty summit. So if any hears
My voice, who dwells upon it, nymph or god,
Shepherd or farmer, or the meanest clod
That lurks among the rocks, attend to me:
40 Whoever finds my cows I swear shall be
Rewarded richly. Harken to my word!
I am Apollo! – and I've lost my herd!

Enter SILENUS *the Satyr with great haste and self-importance.*

SILENUS:
    Great Lord Apollo, tell me why and how
You chance to be in trouble. Though I'm now
Well gone in years, I hurried – simply ran,
As you can see – to help you. If I can
Do anything, friend Phoebus, to assist
You in your trouble, don't let me be missed
From a friend's place beside you. Undismayed,
50 Count now on me, I'll help you – if I'm paid.
So tell me what makes dark your shining brows.

APOLLO:
Some clever thief has stolen all my cows.

SILENUS:
I'll send my sharp-eyed sons without delay
To seek for them – provided that you pay.

APOLLO:
I praise your zeal – if you bring back my cows.

SILENUS:
  Thanks for your praise – if you fulfil your vows.
APOLLO (*grandly*):
  Gold waits the finder whosoe'er it be.
SILENUS:
  Gold did you say? I hope the finder's me!
APOLLO:
  I'll set a wreath, besides, upon your head.
SILENUS:
  No good to us. What can you give instead?   60
APOLLO:
  I'll offer that for which all creatures seek.
SILENUS:
  Go on – What is the gift of which you speak?
APOLLO:
  Freedom from toil for you and all your sons.
SILENUS:
  That's something like! I'll tell the boys at once.
  (*Shouting*) Come here, you lads, I'm on to something
      good,
  An easy job, with pay, well understood!

                Enter CHORUS OF SATYRS.

FIRST SATYR:
  Here we are, father! Always close at hand!
  An easy job, you say – with cash? How grand!
SILENUS:
  Both gold and freedom here Apollo vows
  To us if we can find his stolen cows.   70

                Exit APOLLO *with slow dignity.*

CHORUS:
  Hurrah for the herdsmen of Phoebus Apollo
    By misty mountain and gloomy glen!
  Silenus, lead, and your sons will follow
  Over the mountain from summit to hollow,
    Under the mountain, and back again!

Search the wilderness, cave and cavern,
   Search the cities where men abide;
Our feet shall echo in town and tavern,
Through hut and hall as we roam and raven,
80   Combing Hellas from side to side.

Lord Apollo be ever near to us
   Follow our labours by fell and fold,
Making the quest of your cows more clear to us,
Urging us on, oh god most dear to us,
   You whose wallet is lined with gold!

SILENUS:

O Gods, O Fortune, and the Heavenly Guide
Show me the cows, wherever they may hide;
Be my quest short, and little labour cost
The finding of the cattle that were lost
90 Or stolen, plundered, looted from this god.
    Here, wake up, you (*to the audience*) I say!
                    Don't dare to nod,
But tell me straight, has any one of you
Heard, seen, or smelt the cows? The slightest clue
Will win a gracious glance from Phoebus' eyes,
For you, his thanks and mine; for us, the prize.
So don't be shy, but come right up and tell
Where in the world – or out of it – they dwell.

CHORUS:

That would be luck, which I hope may befall
Us now. Then we'd not need to hunt at all!

A SATYR:

100 There's someone getting up! You, down below!

SILENUS:

Anyone? Someone? What, does *no* one know?
Why then, it's high time that I set to work.
Now Satyrs, to the job, don't dare to shirk!

Nose to the ground – that's right! – to catch the scent
Borne on the wind from where the cattle went.
Down on your knees, bent double, follow close
The track that leads you, or the scent that blows;
Search well and widely, do not fear to bend –
Of search and satyr let us see the end!

SATYRS:

A god, a god, a god! Hip-hip-hurray!   110
I think we'll find them now without delay.

FIRST SATYR:

A trace! A trace! Just here a cow has trod!

SECOND SATYR:

Don't shout so loudly – you'll offend the god.

FIRST SATYR:

Sorry I spoke! If Phoebus heard, he might
Say that our methods were not strictly right!

SECOND SATYR:

You fellows over there, what have you found?

THIRD SATYR:

Proof positive: some footsteps on the ground.

FOURTH SATYR:

Look! Look! Some hoof-marks over there again!

FIFTH SATYR:

And here another, printed clear and plain.

SATYRS:

Let's scatter; if the cows are somewhere near,   120
Surely their lowing will reach someone's ear.

Sound of a lyre begins off stage very softly.

FIRST SATYR:

I still can't catch a bovine sound at all!
Would the cows come, d'you think, if I should call?

SECOND SATYR:

These *are* their footsteps – we just need to hunt.

THIRD SATYR:

Good gracious, look! These tracks are back to front!
Just look at that, the hoof-marks are reversed!
What can it mean? I think the cows are cursed.
What nightmare order! Front is now the rear:
These point two ways at once ... The tracks are clear,
130 But sure the driver must be mad, or drunk!

*The lyre sounds more loudly, and the Satyrs show
signs of panic.*

SILENUS:

I say, what's up now? Has your courage shrunk?
Running away from nothing! You'll not make
Good huntsmen, writhing there just like a snake
Flat on your bellies; what new dodge is this?
It's got no point at all, or one I miss!
Get up, you look like hedge-hogs without feet,
Crouching and crawling like an ape on heat!
It all seems daft. I only wish I knew
Who'd taught you this mad dance – explain it, do.

CHORUS:

140 Ou! Ou! Ou! Ah! Ah! Ou! Ah! Ou! Boo! Hoo!

SILENUS:

What are you howling for? Who's scaring you?
What have you seen? It's surely not a ghost?
Why do you dance like a mad Maenad host?
I can hear nothing anywhere around –
Except a very distant scraping sound
It can't be *that*! Speak! Have you been struck dumb?

CHORUS:

Listen!

SILENUS:

What should I hear, when you're all mum?

CHORUS:

Listen, I say!

SILENUS:

        You're really a disgrace
Scaring yourselves, not helping in the chase.

CHORUS:

      Hush, keep still, and you will hear   150
         What so fills our hearts with awe;
      Drives us almost mad with fear –
         Sound no mortal heard before!

SILENUS:

Why should that faint noise scare you? Tell me why
You stand like statues, pointing to the sky?
You worthless beasts, you see, I do declare,
Ghosts in each shadow, bogies everywhere!
You're useless, spineless, lacking in all trust,
Mere lumps of talk, and carrion, and lust:
You boast about your courage every day   160
And when the crisis comes, you run away.
But I, your father, I, you worthless breed,
When I was young, I was a man indeed!
The nymphs I conquered! and the deeds I did!
I *led* the battles, never went and hid;
Nor screamed when I heard cattle on a hill
Like some that I could name. My glory still
Shines bright, and you would tarnish it with fear
Because some shepherd's cunning cry you hear.
Scared like a baby by an unknown sound   170
You cast Apollo's riches on the ground;
Have you forgotten gold, and freedom too,
Promised by him to me as well as you?
Well, give it up then; go and hide in bed …
    You blethering cowards, I'll punch you on the head,
I'll make you sore and sorry if you don't
Get back to work. Now who dares say he won't?

CHORUS:

    Get in front, don't skulk behind,
     Then we'll see who's scared, who's not!
180   Come and lead us, then you'll find
     That you're talking rot!

SILENUS:

 Never you fear, I'll come and show you how
 A valiant hunter ought to chase a cow.
 You'll dilly-dally there the whole day through;
 I'll just drop in, and show you what to do!

 SILENUS *attempts to restore order forcibly among the Satyrs,*
  who dance and sing as they try to avoid him.

CHORUS:

 Pish! Tush! Whoop-la – and away!
  Say what is the matter with you?
 Strutting and butting, and shouting and pouting,
 Dancing and prancing – now really I'm doubting
190 If there's one word of truth that you say
  Or one little deed that you do!

FIRST SATYR:

   Help me quick – he's caught me bending!

SECOND SATYR:

   Oh, he's caught you, sure enough.

FIRST SATYR:

   Help I say, he's tearing, rending –

SECOND SATYR:

   Go it, father – that's the stuff!

CHORUS:

 Come now, were you really so gay,
  Old man, in the days of your youth?
 Dashing and slashing, such mighty blows lavishing;
 Chasing and facing, and raping and ravishing –
200 Just think now, and surely you'll say
  That your fancy is painting the truth!

THIRD SATYR:

     Help me quick – his nails are tearing!

FOURTH SATYR:

     Glad it isn't me, but you!

THIRD SATYR:

     Look, his eyes are red and glaring:

FOURTH SATYR:

     Stop it, father – that'll do!

SILENUS:

Now will you please obey me, and not dare
To kick your silly legs up in the air?

SATYRS:

Of course we will, but what about the sound?
It faded when we started dancing round.

SILENUS:

It never did exist, save in your head –   210

FIRST SATYR:

Which now you've hit and made to buzz instead!

SECOND SATYR:

Hush! Just a minute … There it is again.
Now listen, father, and you'll hear it plain.

SILENUS:

I can't hear anything … At least I thought
I heard a … Tush, there's nothing of the sort!

FIRST SATYR:

You're silent … Do we speak the truth or not?
Surely you hear it! Are you deaf, or what?

SILENUS:

Shut up a moment … (*Sound of the lyre becomes louder.*)

FIRST SATYR:

     What?

SILENUS:

                        I mustn't stay –
Something I've got to do ...

FIRST SATYR:

                    Don't go away!

SILENUS:

220   I really must ... Important date ... But you
Can stay and find the cows, and earn the screw
And get rich quick. I'm sorry I can't wait –
I'm wasting time ... Goodbye ... Important date ...

CHORUS:

Not if we know it! Sneaking away,
    Leaving us all in the lurch like that!
Here you are, and with us you stay
    To see this through to the end – that's flat!

There's someone there, we must get him out!
    Some robber chief in a cavern lies!
230   Now, Silenus, suppose you shout,
    And find the cattle, and win the prize!

Louder still! Will he never come?
    Beat the ground, and bellow again:
He may be deaf, but we're far from dumb!
    One more yell, boys, with might and main!

Enter the Nymph KYLLENE *from the Cave.*

KYLLENE:

What rough beasts are these? What is it that brings,
This clamour here to frighten the wild things?
What do you seek, so changed from when, of old,
You were good subjects of Silenus' fold;
240   When, armed with thyrsus, clad in fawn-skin, you
Led out the dance in Dionysus' view,
Singing the chant divine amid the rout
Of revelling nymphs that follow him about?

Whence is your present madness, whence the change
That sends you screaming in a dance so strange?
I heard a call, like hunters in the wood,
Near to the lair where lies some wolfish brood,
Raised in defiant hate; and then a cry
Of thieves and rapine echoed to the sky!
'Reward', 'a proclamation', 'cows' – and then   250
Your words grew turgid, and above my den
The stamp of feet that shook the earth around,
And one continuous roar of crazy sound.
How could I stay then in my mountain cave?
I come in fear, a harmless nymph, and crave
Protection: tell me now, what will befall
This foolish girl who has obeyed your call?

CHORUS:

> Stay your anger, stately lady,
>   Not in strife and war come we
> To your bower so deep and shady,   260
>   But your careful friends to be.
>
> Then assail us not with taunting,
>   But the secret now disclose
> Of the music, lovely, daunting,
>   That from out this hill arose.

KYLLENE:

Come, that's a gentler manner than before:
Hunting like this you'll surely find much more
Than you could ever gain in violent-wise,
Scaring poor nymphs, and yelling to the skies.
Quarrels and arguments are of one breed,   270
So tell me calmly what it is you need.

CHORUS:

Kyllene, queen of all these mountains high,
We'll tell you what we came for by and by;

But first explain to us, this sound which quite
Sets our poor teeth on edge – but not with fright.

KYLLENE:

Know first: if you reveal what I relate
Some ghastly punishment will be your fate
And bow you down with suffering and woe.
   Now for my secret: Satyrs, you must know
That Hera, Heaven's queen is swiftly stirred
To jealousy – a fact I'm sure you've heard!
Now Zeus – who likes his fling from time to time –
Sought this fair cave in the Arcadian clime,
Where Maia, child of Atlas, dwelt that day;
And in her arms all night the Thunderer lay,
Unknown to Hera. Of that union came
An only son – and Hermes is his name.
But Maia, wasted sore with labour pain,
Might not attend the baby, but was fain
To choose a nurse: that office I perform,
By day and night keeping this infant warm,
Bending above his cradle to supply
   Both food and drink to him. The days go by
And every morn he grows beyond compare:
It is but six days since his mother bare
The wondrous child, and yet he grows so fast
Each day, that childhood is already past
And he begins to blossom into youth.
Such is the child I foster; and in truth
We do but hide him by his father's will.
   As for the sound that scared you from the hill,
Ringing from hands unseen, mysterious, fay –
The child invented it this very day,
Out of an upturned shell: that is as near
As I can come to name it. What you hear
Comes from an animal that lately died,
Yet still is full of music. Deep inside

280

290

300

The hollow cavern now the baby plays
Upon the wondrous thing; and strange amaze
Falls upon all who hear him, even as you   310
Were scared when harmony unknown and new
First fell upon your ears. But Maia's son
Plays happily – as if in childish fun –
Resting in the deep cave. You need not dread
A baby playing on a creature dead.

SILENUS:

I can't believe that any beasts make music when they die!

KYLLENE:

You must believe the words I say. A goddess does not lie.

SILENUS:

So loud a voice could never swell from beast whose life
was done.

KYLLENE:

It's true, though: it sings loud in death, that, living, voice
had none.

SILENUS:

Was this same creature in its life long, curved, or fat or
thin?   320

KYLLENE:

Short like a gourd, all shrivelled up, with spots upon its
skin.

SILENUS:

I know! I know! It must have been a panther or a cat.

KYLLENE:

Quite, quite unlike, with little legs, with body round and
fat.

SILENUS:

What, like a weasel, or a crab? At least its shape is plain.

KYLLENE:

No, not like either in the least: you'd better guess again.

SILENUS:

I know! A beetle! Such a one as Etna's slopes may boast!

KYLLENE:

Well done! Well done! You've guessed at last what it
resembles most.

SILENUS:

But is the noise inside or out? The method of it tell.

KYLLENE:

It is the crust that makes the notes, exactly like a shell.

SILENUS:

330 What does he call it, tell us quick – this baby in the byre?

KYLLENE:

He calls the beast a Tortoise, and the instrument a Lyre.

SILENUS:

But tell us how a hollow shell can make a noise like that.

KYLLENE:

He's covered all the hollow in, to make it smooth and
flat.

SILENUS:

What, you don't mean the beast's alive, imprisoned in
the shell?

KYLLENE:

He scraped it out, the beast is dead, as you have heard me
tell.

SILENUS:

Then what's he got across the crust, and which thing
makes the sound?

KYLLENE:

He stretched a skin across the shell, and fastened it all
round.

SILENUS:

And what's he used to cover it? The pelt of this same
thing?

KYLLENE:

A piece of ox-hide, newly flayed, a piece of gut for string.

SILENUS:

Indeed this sounds a wondrous toy: we've very glad we
    came.   340

KYLLENE:

But to disturb us as you did, I really call a shame.
To make this fuss about a toy, invented by a lad,
The only comfort that he has to cheer him when he's sad,
For you must know that he delights to sing like creature
    crazed,
And play upon the lyre and hum to tunes that he has
    raised
With subtle difference from each note. But I've been
    here too long –
And I have told you how this boy drew from the dead a
    song.

CHORUS:

        Sweet, sweet is the voice of the lyre
            As its music floats over the land,
        Weaving fancies, string-born, that inspire   350
            All around, at a touch of the hand.

        Oh, granted the music's divine,
            But what I am trying to say
        Is that we have a proof and a sign
            That the thief we are hunting today

        Is this godling, whoever he be,
            Who has fashioned this exquisite toy;
        Now pray don't be angry with me!
            It's our duty, not done to annoy.

KYLLENE:

Now really that's the silliest thing I've heard;   360
A charge of theft! It's rather too absurd!

SILENUS:

  I swear I hate to say it, lady, but –

KYLLENE:

  To call a god a thief! You *are* a mutt!

SILENUS:

  Yes, I said thief! I wish I'd been in time …

KYLLENE:

  To see your folly? Well, it's quite sublime!

SILENUS:

  To catch this trickster in the very act.

KYLLENE:

  The catcher would be caught, and that's a fact.

SILENUS:

  He stole the cows, and he must pay the cost.

KYLLENE:

  Really? And what besides? I feel quite lost …

SILENUS:

370 He's killed an ox, and skinned it, don't you see!

KYLLENE:

  His brother's cow? It surely cannot be!

SILENUS:

  He took the herd of cattle right away –

KYLLENE:

  A child who hasn't seen his seventh day!
  This is too much, and well I understand
  That all this folly is some trick you've planned;
  Some silly trick. You're full of them, I know,
  But henceforth, if it really must be so,
  If you enjoy buffoonery, or believe
  That it will profit you, I give you leave
380 To laugh at me as much as you see fit –
  I'll just not notice you the slightest bit!

Only I warn you, don't miscall a child
Whose sire is surely Zeus; nor make these wild
And foolish accusations against one
Who's only known six days beneath the sun!
Moreover, you can't say it comes by kind,
And he inherits vice: you will not find
Great Zeus to be a thief, nor yet the kin
Of Maia, Atlas' daughter steeped in sin.
Therefore begone, and seek your thief elsewhere   390
For no lean harvest tempts to thieving here,
And poverty does not invade this home.
Think of his parentage before you come
To fix a crime on him: it isn't right
Or proper. But you always have been quite
A child in your behaviour: you forget
That you're a man full grown, and you would yet
Skip like a saucy ram among the ewes,
It's wrong a bald-pate coot like you should choose
To ape the gambols of an amorous goat.   400
The gods bring fools to harm, I'd have you note.

CHORUS:

      Cunning tales of double meaning
        Twisted council, clever word!
      But our judgement still is leaning
        To the verdict you have heard.

      It is he, how sure we're feeling,
        He who made the stately lyre,
      Got the cow-hide by his stealing
        Cattle from Apollo's byre.

      No more twisting, nor evasion,   410
        Never knit those lovely brows!
      Sure, in spite of your persuasion,
        This young Hermes stole the cows!

KYLLENE:

The things you've said; the names that you have used!
Gods don't stand calmly by to be abused.

SILENUS:

But he's a villain, if he acts like one.

KYLLENE:

You should not dare to slander Zeus's son.

SILENUS:

What would you have me say, if not the truth?

KYLLENE:

Such words as these are foolish and uncouth.

SILENUS:

420   He stole the cattle! You cannot deny
That Hermes when he lately wished to ply
The craft of music-maker used the hide
Of a slain ox! The rest he has inside
The hollow cavern, or beneath some hill
In a wild valley that's more distant still.
I say you can't deny it: only think;
How clear the proof is; and that I would shrink
From charging gods with theft without good cause.

KYLLENE:

He hasn't got a single cow indoors!

SILENUS:

430   Why then, he's put them somewhere else instead.

KYLLENE:

You'll find them straying, waiting to be fed!

SILENUS:

Yes, hidden away – and Hermes knows the place!

KYLLENE:

How will you prove *he* set them out to graze?

SILENUS:

We've enough proof to catch the thief, I say.

KYLLENE:
  Villain! What thief has stolen these cows away?

SILENUS:
  The child you talk of – he I'm sure's the one.

KYLLENE:
  Again I say, don't slander Zeus's son.

SILENUS:
  I'll stop the moment you produce the child.

KYLLENE:
  You and your cattle really make me wild.

SILENUS:
  Suppose you send this lad you speak of here.   440

KYLLENE:
  One can't command immortals to appear.

SILENUS:
  Then tell him we bear news, if he would deign …

KYLLENE:
  News of what kind, I beg you to explain.

SILENUS:
  A message from his brother-god, who vows
  Dire vengeance on the thief who stole his cows,
  But rich rewards for any who can tell
  Where in the world these errant cattle dwell.

KYLLENE:
  So Lord Apollo's hired you for this quest,
  And pays you well! I really might have guessed
  That such an ancient lazy thing as you,   450
  All fat and lechery, would not pursue
  This arduous duty without some good cause.

SILENUS:
  Fair nymph, suppose you enter by those doors
  And tell the child before it is too late;
  Say that Apollo calls him to the gate –

75

The order comes from him: now don't you see
How serious this quarrel soon may be?
Unless the boy explains, I have no doubt
That a new war in heaven will break out.

KYLLENE:

460   I will do this. But you have been too bold:
I would not be *you* for all Phoebus' gold!

         KYLLENE *goes into the Cave.*

CHORUS:

There once was a war in the heavenly halls
    In the reign of King Cronos the old;
The true gods rejoice when a Titan falls
Down, down to the brass Tartarean walls
    That round their dread prison enfold.
          What if Apollo
        Makes war, red war
With the Hermes child who has stolen his kine?
470   And we must follow
        Through fresh warm gore
In danger and sorrow to peak and pine?

Oh, give us the hills where the Maenads dance
    In the train of the Bromian king;
Let us kick up our heels as we caper and prance,
As we cast on each maiden an amorous glance
    And gleefully gambol and sing!
         Would we were drinking
        The juice of the grape,
480   Till the earth span round and the sky came down:
        For now we are thinking
        Of some dread shape,
Some angry god with death in his frown.

    Help and protect us now,
      Good father Silenus;

How I hate the name of cow!
And will ever hate it, I vow.
   The god draws near in his rage;
   Unkind battle he'll wage:
He is seeking for vengeance now!   490
   Why must it have been us!

Enter HERMES *from the Cave, young and innocent-looking,*
    but with a merry twinkle in his eyes.

HERMES:

As I lay sleeping in the quiet gloom
There came harsh sounds of discord and of doom
Outside the cavern, and I quaked in fear,
Not knowing what dread enemy was near.
Then came my nurse Kyllene where I lay
All swaddled in my cradle, and straightway
Bade me arise and hasten to the light
Where messengers called for me. In a fright
I sprang from bed, though but a child new-born   500
And hastened out into the light of morn
To see what these things were. For how am I
Even to name the creatures passing by?

CHORUS:

A fair, tall stripling for but six days' life:
Yet no strong thief to be the cause of strife!

SILENUS:

Now look here sir, we don't want any fuss
About this business. We have called you thus
Before us to accuse you of a deed
Of dreadful villainy: you'll never speed
In your young life if you begin like this!   510
It happened that Apollo chanced to miss
His herd of cattle from the Doric land
Where they were left to graze. You understand

How much he loves his cows? Well now their theft
Has made him simply wild. In haste he left
The halls of heaven, and sped by land and sea
To seek them out. It chanced with us to be
Nearby on mount Kyllene, and to hear
His proclamation; so we all drew near
520 The shining one – I'm an old friend of his –
And any trouble, I assured him, is
Felt just as much by me. Well, he has gone
Questing towards Tegea all alone,
Leaving us here behind to search this place
For the lost cows. Now I have chanced to trace
The theft at once to you: I've caught the thief!
Such cleverness as mine's beyond belief!

HERMES:

You strange, wild man, so hairy and so rough,
Do please stop talking, you've said quite enough
530 To puzzle my poor brain: I really can't
Imagine what on earth it is you want.

SILENUS:

We want Apollo's cows, and you know well
Where on the earth, or under it, they dwell.

HERMES:

What is a cow? I've only heard them named!
Surely you're joking: how can I be blamed,
A child of six days old – although I've grown
As well becomes a god, I'm sure you'll own.
    And why should I steal cows? I do not care
For things like that; nor wander anywhere
540 But in my cavern home. All I desire
Is to lie snugly down beside the fire;
Or for my nurse to bathe and cherish me,
Feed me with pap, and dandle cunningly

Until I fall asleep. It's most absurd
That I'd steal cows – of which I'd never heard
Until you mentioned them a while ago.
    But now I'll swear, if you will have it so,
A mighty oath by the Infernal Lake,
The oath that no immortal god may break –
I have not stolen things I've never seen   550
Called cows: my cave and conscience are both clean!

SILENUS:

Good gracious me! This youngster would convince
The oldest councillor, or the wisest prince!
One could believe you'd been a thief for years;
And really, to my judgement it appears
You've lied about your age! If at six days
You've done all this, it fills me with amaze
To think what deeds you'll do in time to come!
However, all true gods strike mortals dumb.
    But still, I'll swear you stole away the kine   560
Of great Apollo – also god divine –
And led them this way, past the cavern mouth,
And kept them here – or drove them from the south
Across this open place. The northward ground
Is rocky, and no footsteps can be found
Upon it, but they're plain enough just here;
Although confused, the main direction's clear.

HERMES:

I think you must have had a nasty dream
And don't know which things are, and which things
     seem.   570
You say the cows were driven to the north,
But you just said Apollo first set forth
From that direction: he'd have seen them then,
Or heard about them somewhere among men.

CHORUS:
There's certainly some sense in this remark,
And, to speak truth, I'm still quite in the dark.

SILENUS:
You stole the cows, wherever they may be!

HERMES:
What makes you try to fix the deed on me?

SILENUS:
That instrument you've got beneath your arm ...

HERMES:
Is called a lyre; I made it, where's the harm?

SILENUS:
580   Now tell me how you did it, with what art ...

HERMES:
I used a tortoise for the lower part.

SILENUS:
Yes, and I grant you that explains the shell.

HERMES:
I'm pleased to find you understand so well.

SILENUS:
My! You were clever to devise it so!

HERMES:
Yes, I've got brains! I'm glad you fellows know.

SILENUS:
But what can make the hollow vessel sound?

HERMES:
This piece of ox-hide fastened down all round.

SILENUS:
Now tell me where you got that strip of hide!

HERMES:
The skin? I found it – picked it up inside.

SILENUS:
I don't believe it! That skin's newly flayed!   590

HERMES:
What does it mean? That funny word you said?

SILENUS:
We've caught you now, whatever you pretend.

HERMES:
I think this interview had better end.
It's really time I had a little doze.
A child needs lots of sleep – for then he grows.

SILENUS:
You've grown enough, my lad. Don't think to fly!
Wait here, Apollo's coming by and by!

HERMES:
I'm really not prepared for callers now:
Tell him to come again, when times allow.

SILENUS:
I've got you, and don't mean to let you go   600
Apollo will pay well for this, I know!

HERMES:
Just as you like; provided he comes soon.
And if you're quiet I'll play a little tune.

He plays on the lyre.

CHORUS (*dancing more and more wildly*):
When the sound of the lyre
Gets hold of my heels,
All my body takes fire
Till it staggers and reels
Away and away to the madding sweet sound,
Till our bodies grow wearied and sink to the ground.

610
  Not the juice of the grape
   As it foams down my throat;
  Not as oft the soft shape
   Of a wood-nymph I note;
 Not the fume of the wine nor the thrill of desire
 Sends me mad with delight like the sound of the lyre.

  Now my feet cannot cease
   Nor my legs be at rest
  For the wild strains increase,
   And increases my zest,
620
 I long not for love, and I crave not for wine –
 Let me live, let me die with this music divine.

FIRST SATYR:

Stay the wild dance! Apollo's drawing near,
And all this shady business will grow clear.

  Enter APOLLO *eagerly.*

APOLLO:

I have returned, my friends, with news indeed!
I come from Tegea now in breathless speed
Where, in a ditch, I found an ancient man
Called Battus, who revealed the villain's plan.
For he had seen, he said, a comely youth
Drawing my cows behind him from the south.
Oh wondrous cunning, insolence divine!
630
For this same stripling urged the frightened kine
To shamble backwards – dragged them by the tail!
Moreover as he strove his best to hale
The unwilling cows behind him, Battus said,
The youngling's feet were strangely basketed
With willow slivers and with osier boughs,
That none might trace the herdsman or the cows.
 And so I found the cattle: but alas,
A far more dreadful thing had come to pass,

For two of them, two of my precious cows,
Lay slain: the flesh on twelve new heaps of boughs   640
Burned up in offering to us gods on high.
    It makes me mad to think my cows should die
Beneath this villain's hand! And now I swear
My vengeance shall be great, and wondrous rare!

      He stops, gasping for breath, and fans himself.

CHORUS:

        To slay the lord Apollo's kine
          Is really most outrageous!
        We hope that you'll impose a fine,
        Imprisonment – and most condign
        Reproaches on the wicked thief
        Whose deed, though vile beyond belief,   650
        Is clever – we might say divine –
          And really most courageous!

APOLLO (*at his most petulant*):
        I do not think it in the least
        A clever trick to make a feast
        Of stolen cattle – which are mine!
        Impiety to gods divine
          Is certain to enrage us!

CHORUS:

But see whom we have here: the villain vile
Who stole the cows, and hid them by his guile.

APOLLO:

Is this the fellow? This same callow lad?   660
He looks too young and feeble. You are mad
To charge him with the theft. Yet stay awhile,
Just let me look ... Yes! Something in that smile,
Those curls ambrosial ... What *will* Hera say!
There *was* a rumour Zeus was seen to stray
Disguised down here on earth, the other day ...

      He chuckles to himself.

CHORUS:

Although he has stolen your cows,
  Great Phoebus Apollo,
The glory that shines from his brows
670 Is a proof that his birth was divine ...
And indeed you come both of one line,
Though your father paid various vows.
  (I'm sure that you follow?)

HERMES:

Oh, what's all this chatter to me?
It's as wild as the waves of the sea
That break on the shingle all day.
I'll listen no longer, but play
  On my lyre, Lord Apollo.

  HERMES *plays on the lyre.*

CHORUS:

Ah, when I hear the music of the lyre
680 I long to dance and dance! I'm filled with fire!

APOLLO:

Fair stranger, all my soul is sick with joy:
What is this witching art that you employ?

SILENUS:

Hear me, good Lord Apollo, hear me quick!
Don't listen to the lyre, it's all a trick
To make you pardon him the stolen kine!
This instrument, although it seems divine,
Proves his sure guilt beyond the slightest doubt!

APOLLO:

What crack-brain theory are you bringing out?

SILENUS:

The lyre in his hand! Examine well.

APOLLO:

690 A clever thing made of a tortoise shell.

84

SILENUS:

Yes, but what else is used? Look closely please.

APOLLO:

Why do you ask me questions such as these?

SILENUS:

Oh do look close! What shuts the hollow in?

APOLLO:

Why all this fuss about a piece of skin?

SILENUS:

It's just that skin! It once was on a cow!

APOLLO:

Oh, I begin to see your meaning now!

CHORUS (*jogging up and down excitedly*):

  Forgive him, Lord Phoebus, please!
   We want some more music!
  There were never such tunes as these,
  They give youth to our backs and our knees!   700
   They don't, surely, make you sick?

APOLLO:

  They should, but they don't! I'm on fire!
   I'm enchanted! I'm fay!
  Though a god, I'm enslaved – by the lyre!
  Is it magic, this breathless desire
   To make music all day?

SILENUS:

I long to join the song and dance divine –
But, Phoebus, what about the stolen kine?
And what about the gold you promised us
If our detective work were prosperous?   710

APOLLO:

There's truth in that! Young man, what do you say?
You stole my cows: I think you ought to pay;
Reward this person, and make up to me
The loss of those you killed so wickedly.

HERMES:

    Apollo, brother of the shining dart,
    Why should such quarrels sever heart from heart?
    Here and before you all, I swear by Styx
    Never again to play Apollo tricks,
    Never to steal from him, nor make him cross.
720   And now, as I can't quite repair his loss
    (A cow once dead can scarcely graze again),
    I'll see if I can soothe my brother's pain.
      Apollo, this my lyre I bestow
    On you for ever. May sweet music flow
    Beneath your hand eternally divine,
    And high Parnassus ever be the shrine
    Of all fair song. Round the Castalian spring
    Notes of Apollo's lyre for ever cling!

CHORUS:

    All well and good, but what of our reward?
730   Apollo, you were always a just lord!

APOLLO:

    You shall be free, according to my word.
    And when the music of my lyre is heard,
    The madness of delight, of sweet desire
    Shall so possess you with its wondrous fire
    That all dull things forgetting, you shall be
    Swung to the fairest heights of ecstasy!

        Now hark to Apollo
          Who plays on his lyre!
        Come follow, come follow
740   To seek your desire.

        With music delighting
          The children of day,
        Apollo is lighting
          The world on its way.

        Exit, playing on the lyre.

CHORUS:

    Apollo, Apollo is speeding and leading
      The dance of my days out by valley and hill;
  Sweet, sweet the desire in my heart that is breeding;
      I gasp with delight as the lyre sounds shrill:
  I follow Apollo his leading, go speeding
      Away and away he is leading me still!   750

        Exeunt, dancing.

NOTES TO *The Searching Satyrs*

THE date of the *Ichneutai* is uncertain; its genuineness as a work of Sophocles is proved beyond doubt by a passage from the play quoted by Athenaeus (ii. 62). Various periods in the career of Sophocles have been put forward by scholars, but no conclusive proof is available; it may be assigned most probably to an early date, and is perhaps not much later than *Antigone*, which was produced about 440 B.C.

The scene is before a cave on Mount Kyllene in the North of the Peloponnese, and in this, as in the introduction of the nymph of that mountain in place of Maia the mother of Hermes, in the placing of the theft of the cattle before the making of the lyre, and, of course, in the introduction of the Satyrs, the play differs from the Homeric Hymn to Hermes, which it follows fairly closely in most other details. The best translation of the Hymn is that into prose by Andrew Lang (*Allen and Unwin*, 1899), whose introductory essay on the Legend and its parallels in Folklore is of considerable interest. Shelley also made a pleasant rendering of the Hymn in verse.

Line 4, etc. The cows of Apollo were among his most traditional possessions, and are probably identical with the Cattle of the Sun killed and eaten by the followers of Odysseus.

Lines 21 to 34. This traces Apollo's journey in search of the cattle, whose traditional grazing ground was in Thessaly.

Line 63. Freedom from toil for you and all your sons. This line has caused considerable difficulties to various scholars: whose slaves were the Satyrs that Apollo proposes to free them? Possibly they were his own slaves (as Pearson suggests): they would traditionally be the servants of Dionysus; but Euripides makes them the slaves of Polyphemus in *The Cyclops* without any difficulty.

Line 125. These tracks are back to front. In the Homeric Hymn, Hermes seems to have dragged the cows backwards by their tails so that the tracks should lead in the wrong direction, and to have worn on his own feet sandals made of osiers to disguise his footprints. Apollodorus (*Library*, iii. x. 2), however, says that he bound shoes on the cattle's feet also.

Lines 239 to 243, etc. The association of the Satyrs with the Nymphs dates from Hesiod, who, in a fragment quoted by Strabo (x. 471), says that from the daughters of Hecaterus 'were born the divine mountain Nymphs, and the tribe of worthless, helpless Satyrs.'

Line 284. Maia. She was one of the Pleiades, the daughters of Atlas the Titan and of Pleione daughter of Ocean.

Lines 316 to 347. In the Greek these lines are in the metre called *iambic tetrameter acatalectic*, not otherwise known in Greek tragedy or comedy, though to be found in the lyric fragments of Alcman and Alcaeus. I have sought to translate them here in a corresponding English metre.

Lines 440 to 750. The mutilated text of the play ends at line 439, and from then onwards I have reconstructed, using the Homeric Hymn as my main source.

Lines 462, etc. The chorus compares the possible war that may break out between Apollo and Hermes with the old battle between the Gods and Titans.

Line 523. Tegea: a town between Kyllene and the plain of Sparta, in mythological times the home of Atalanta and her descendants, such as Promachus who fought at Troy.

Line 627. Battus: the informer from the Homeric Hymn; he is not mentioned by Apollodorus.

Line 723. The Homeric Hymn gives the exchange of the lyre for the cattle, as does Apollodorus, who besides credits Hermes with the invention of pipes, which Apollo exchanges with him for his golden wand. Alcaeus elaborates the tale, making Hermes steal Apollo's bow, which he only returns when the golden wand, his symbol as a Herald, is given to him. The fragments from Alcaeus may be rendered as follows:

> Oh ruler of Kyllene, hail!
>   To sing unto thee is my will
> Whom Maia bare, so runs the tale,
>   Upon that windy hill.

*

And when thou there hadst stolen away
   The oxen of the Archer King,
He knew by magic, and straightway
   Came to thee threatening.

But thou didst steal his very bow,
   Whereat he smiled and gave to thee
His golden wand, that men might know
   Thy rule of heraldry.

NOTE

While my translation of *The Cyclops* appears here in print for the first time, *The Searching Satyrs* was published in 1946 by Edmund Ward, then of Leicester, in a limited edition of 550 numbered copies printed on hand-made paper: this version has been revised considerably and in places re-translated for the present volume.

R. L. G.

APPENDIX

Two Dithyrambs

Both Tragedy and Satyr Play are supposed to have
originated in the Dithyramb which was a choric song
and dance in honour of Dionysus. Unfortunately
no early Dithyrambs have survived, nor any of a
Satyric character.

Two of the earliest examples are by Pindar, and
in spite of their Dionysiac intention they can hardly
be described as licentious or undignified. Their
connection with the chorus of a Satyr play is, however, apparent, and it seems worth including them
here as affording an interesting side-light on the
Satyric tradition.

I

A Dithyramb for the Thebans

From lips of men in olden days
    The Dithyramb
Flowed forth in curious, lengthy lays;
    But from new gateways now advance
    The sacred circles of the dance.
And wise are they who know the ways
    The Gods within the heavenly halls
    Perform their Bacchic festivals
    Beneath the glance
Of royal Zeus. The golden jamb
And roof-tree gleam about the place
    Where the Great Mother smiles upon
    The timbrels whirled in unison,
The ringing rattle's race.

There too the Naiad Nymphs lament;
    The frenzied cry
Of dancers with their white necks bent
    Rings out amid the tossing throng;
    The bolts that to great Zeus belong
Are brandished with their fire unspent;
    The warlike shield of Pallas clear
    Sounds with snakes hissing; and the spear
    The war-brand strong
Of fiery Ares leaps on high.
While Artemis, the maid-alone,
    Comes lightly with yoked lions twain
    To dance in Dionysus' train –
Wild things that are his own.

Me too the Muse has raised to sing
    For Hellas, in words wise and choice:
    And gladly, gladly I rejoice
That these my tributes I may bring

To Thebes, my city, where of old
   There was a bride to Cadmus given,
   Harmonia, by the will of Heaven:
      The mother, she,
      Of Semelē
Of whom high things are told.

A Dithyramb for the Athenians

Oh come to the dance; send your glorious favours,
   Gods of Olympus, to Athens where now
In the heart of the city incense-breathing savours
   Are wafted aloft where, with garland on brow,
Your statues are decked with the flowers that belong
To the violet-sweet springtime, new-culled with a song.

And look upon me, with the joyance of singing
   Sped forward by Zeus to hymn with my lays
The Bromian god with the ivy crown ringing
   The brows we adore; nor to stint of my praise
His father almighty, supreme and divine,
And his mystical mother of Cadmean line.

Clearly are seen the bright symbols of Bacchus
   Whenever the purple-robed Hours lead the Spring
With its nectar-sweet flowers; Oh we never shall lack us
   For roses and violets to twine in the ring
Of our hair, as we dance to the flute's madding sound
In Semelē's honour, with diadem bound.